HOW TO MAKE MONEY

TESTED AND PROVEN GIUDES AND TIPS TO GAINING FINANCIAL FREEDOM

No part of this book should be duplicated or produced without the express permission of the author

Copyright Atuegbu Divine Amuche
© 2023
rights reserved

HOW TO MAKE MONEY

CONTENT

Chapter 1: Introduction
- Understanding the mindset required for making money
- Importance of financial literacy
- Defining goals and creating a plan

Chapter 2: Starting a Business
- Identifying your passion and turning it into a profitable venture
- Creating a business plan and market research
- Understanding the legal and financial aspects of starting a business

Chapter 3: Investing in Stocks and Shares
- Understanding the stock market and how it works
- Learning how to analyze stocks and make informed decisions
- The risks and rewards of investing in stocks

Chapter 4: Investing in Real Estate
- Understanding the real estate market and its potential for profit
- Types of real estate investments and their advantages and disadvantages
- Financing options and property management

Chapter 5: Freelancing and Consulting
- Identifying your skills and marketable services
- Building a client base and setting rates
- Marketing your services effectively

Chapter 6: Online Business and E-commerce
- Understanding the potential of online businesses and e-commerce
- Choosing the right platform and creating a website
- Marketing and advertising strategies

Chapter 7: Creating Passive Income
- Understanding what passive income is and how it works

- Creating income streams through investments and rental properties
- Developing and marketing digital products

Chapter 8: Financial Planning and Budgeting
- Understanding the importance of financial planning and budgeting
- Developing a budget and setting financial goals
- Tracking expenses and managing debt

Chapter 9: Negotiation Skills
- Developing effective negotiation skills for salary, contracts, and deals
- Identifying the other party's needs and interests
- Knowing when to walk away

Chapter 10: Building a Personal Brand
- Understanding the importance of personal branding
- Identifying your unique selling points

- Developing an online presence and reputation

Chapter 11: Networking and Building Connections
- The importance of building connections in business
- Developing a professional network
- Tips for networking effectively

Chapter 12: Conclusion
- Bringing together the various strategies discussed in the book
- Developing a personal plan for making money
- Tips for maintaining success and continuing to grow financially.

CHAPTER 1

INTRODUCTION

Money is an essential aspect of modern life. It provides us with the means to purchase the things we need and want, and it allows us to achieve our goals and aspirations. However, for many people, making money can be a challenge. The world of finance can seem daunting and complicated, and the idea of creating wealth can feel unattainable.

This book, "How to Make Money," is designed to help you navigate the complexities of finance and build a successful financial future. Whether you are starting a business, investing in the stock market, or creating passive income streams, this book provides you with the tools and strategies you need to succced.

Throughout the following chapters, we will explore various ways to make money, including starting a business, investing in stocks and shares, investing in real estate, freelancing and consulting, online business and e-commerce, creating passive income, financial planning and budgeting, negotiation skills, building a personal brand, and networking and building connections.

Each chapter provides practical advice and guidance, along with real-world examples and case studies. By the end of the book, you will have a comprehensive understanding of the strategies and techniques you can use to make money and achieve financial success.

So, whether you are starting from scratch or looking to expand your existing wealth, "How to Make Money" is the perfect guide for anyone looking to build a strong financial foundation and achieve their goals. Let's get started!

UNDERSTANDING THE MINDSET REQUIRED FOR MAKING MONEY

Understanding the mindset required for making money is an essential aspect of achieving financial success. Money is not just about numbers and figures; it is about the way we think and approach our finances. A person's mindset can significantly impact their financial decisions, habits, and outcomes.

Here are some key elements of the mindset required for making money:

Positive attitude: A positive attitude towards money is crucial. Many people have limiting beliefs about money, such as thinking that it is scarce or that it is hard to make. A positive mindset believes that money is abundant and that there are endless opportunities to create wealth. A positive mindset is a crucial aspect of achieving financial success. A positive mindset towards money helps to create a healthy relationship with money and encourages an optimistic outlook towards the future. A positive mindset creates an environment where opportunities are recognized and embraced, and challenges are viewed as temporary setbacks rather than insurmountable obstacles.

Here are some ways to cultivate a positive mindset:

❖ **Gratitude:** Practicing gratitude is an essential aspect of developing a positive mindset. Being grateful for what you have rather than focusing on what you don't have can help you appreciate the abundance in your life. Gratitude creates a positive energy that attracts more positivity and abundance.

❖ **Affirmations:** Affirmations are positive statements that you repeat to yourself to help reprogram your mindset. For example, you can repeat affirmations such as "I am capable of creating wealth," "Money comes easily to me," or "I am worthy of financial abundance." Affirmations can help you change your thoughts and beliefs around money and create a more positive outlook.

❖ **Visualization:** Visualization is a technique that involves creating a mental image of what you want to achieve. Visualization can help you create a positive mindset by allowing you to see yourself achieving your financial goals. By visualizing yourself as successful, you create a sense of confidence and belief in yourself.

❖ **Surround yourself with positivity:** Surrounding yourself with positive people, environments, and messages can help cultivate a positive mindset. Negative influences can affect your mindset and hinder your ability to achieve financial success.

❖ **Celebrate small wins:** Celebrating small wins along the way can help create a positive mindset. Recognizing and celebrating progress can help you stay motivated and encouraged to continue towards your financial goals. By practicing gratitude, affirmations, visualization, surrounding yourself with positivity, and celebrating small wins, you can cultivate a positive mindset towards money and create the foundation for financial abundance.

Creativity and resourcefulness: Successful money-makers have a creative and resourceful mindset. They are always looking for new ways to make money and are not afraid to think outside the box. They are also resourceful in finding solutions to challenges and problems that may arise. Creativity and resourcefulness are important elements of the mindset required for making money. Creative and resourceful people are able to identify and capitalize on opportunities that others may overlook. They are able to think outside the box and come up with innovative solutions to problems.

Here are some ways to cultivate creativity and resourcefulness:

❖ **Embrace a growth mindset:** A growth mindset is the belief that skills and abilities can be developed through hard work and dedication. People with a growth mindset are more likely to take on challenges and try new things. By embracing a growth mindset, you can cultivate creativity and resourcefulness.

❖ **Think outside the box:** To be creative and resourceful, you need to be willing to think outside the box. This means challenging assumptions and considering alternative solutions. You can practice this by brainstorming multiple solutions to a problem, asking "what if" questions, and exploring new ideas.

❖ **Experiment:** Experimenting is a great way to cultivate creativity and resourcefulness. This means trying new things and taking calculated risks. Experimenting allows you to learn from your mistakes and discover what works and what doesn't.

❖ **Learn from others:** Learning from others can help you cultivate creativity and resourcefulness. This means seeking out mentors and role models who can offer guidance and support. You can also learn from your peers and colleagues by networking and collaborating on projects.

❖ **Stay informed:** Staying informed about the latest trends and developments in your industry can help you stay creative and resourceful. This means reading industry publications, attending conferences and events, and following thought leaders on social media.

By embracing a growth mindset, thinking outside the box, experimenting, learning from others, and staying informed, you can cultivate creativity and resourcefulness and take advantage of opportunities to create wealth.

Willingness to take risks: Making money often involves taking risks. The willingness to take calculated risks is essential for financial success. However, it is important to note that successful risk-taking requires a certain level of knowledge and experience. Taking risks means stepping outside of your comfort zone and being willing to try new things, even if they involve some level of uncertainty or potential failure. By taking calculated risks, you can open up opportunities for growth and financial success that may not have been available to you otherwise.

Here are some ways to cultivate a willingness to take risks:

❖ **Evaluate potential risks:** Before taking any risks, it's important to evaluate the potential risks and rewards. This means considering the potential outcomes of different scenarios and weighing the pros and cons of each. By doing your research and thinking through the potential risks, you can make more informed decisions about when and how to take risks.

❖ **Start small:** Taking small risks can help you build up your confidence and comfort level with taking risks. This means starting with low-stakes situations and gradually increasing the level of risk as you become more comfortable. For example, you could try a new investment strategy with a small amount of money before investing larger sums.

❖ **Embrace failure:** Failure is a natural part of taking risks, and it's important to embrace it as a learning opportunity rather than a setback. By reframing failure as a chance to learn and grow, you can reduce the fear of failure and become more willing to take risks.

❖ **Take action:** Taking action is essential for cultivating a willingness to take risks. This means being proactive and seizing opportunities as they arise. By taking action, you can build momentum and gain confidence in your ability to take risks.

❖ **Learn from experience:** Learning from experience is a key component of cultivating a willingness to take risks. This means reflecting on your experiences, analyzing what worked and what didn't, and using that information to make better decisions in the future.
By evaluating potential risks, starting small, embracing failure, taking action, and learning from experience, you can cultivate a willingness to take risks and open up opportunities for financial success.

Persistence and resilience: Making money requires persistence and resilience. There will be setbacks and failures along the way, but successful money-makers keep pushing forward and learn from their mistakes. They view failures as opportunities to learn and grow. Persistence and resilience are important elements of the mindset required for making money. Building wealth requires hard work and dedication, and setbacks are inevitable. Being persistent and resilient means staying focused on your goals and persevering in the face of challenges and obstacles.

Here are some ways to cultivate persistence and resilience:

❖ **Set goals:** Setting clear goals is an important first step in cultivating persistence and resilience. This means identifying specific, measurable goals that align with your values and vision for the future. By setting goals, you can stay focused and motivated even when faced with challenges.

❖ **Stay motivated:** Staying motivated is essential for maintaining persistence and resilience. This means finding ways to stay inspired and energized, whether through daily affirmations, positive self-talk, or surrounding yourself with supportive people.

❖ **Embrace failure:** Failure is a natural part of any pursuit, and it's important to embrace it as a learning opportunity rather than a setback. By reframing failure as a chance to learn and grow, you can reduce the fear of failure and become more resilient in the face of challenges.

❖ **Stay flexible:** Being flexible and adaptable is important for cultivating persistence and resilience. This means being open to new ideas and approaches, and being willing to pivot when necessary. By staying flexible, you can navigate unexpected challenges and continue moving towards your goals.

❖ **Learn from experience:** Learning from experience is a key component of cultivating persistence and resilience. This means reflecting on your experiences, analyzing what worked and what didn't, and using that information to make better decisions in the future.

By setting clear goals, staying motivated, embracing failure, staying flexible, and learning from experience, you can cultivate persistence and resilience and overcome challenges on the path to financial success.

Continuous learning: A growth mindset is essential for making money. Successful money-makers are always learning and staying up-to-date with the latest trends and techniques. They are constantly improving their skills and knowledge. Continuous learning is a critical element of the mindset required for making money. In a rapidly changing world, the ability to learn and adapt is essential for staying competitive and building wealth. Continuous learning means committing to ongoing personal and professional development, and seeking out opportunities to expand your knowledge and skills.

Here are some ways to cultivate a commitment to continuous learning:

❖ **Embrace curiosity:** Cultivating a sense of curiosity is essential for continuous learning. This means staying open to new ideas and perspectives, and seeking out opportunities to learn about topics that interest you.

❖ **Seek out new experiences:** Seeking out new experiences is a great way to expand your knowledge and skills. This means trying new things, whether that's taking a class, attending a conference, or exploring a new hobby.

❖ **Invest in education:** Investing in education is a key component of continuous learning. This means seeking out formal education opportunities, such as degree programs or certifications, as well as informal learning opportunities, such as online courses or workshops.

❖ **Read widely:** Reading is an important way to expand your knowledge and perspective. This means reading widely, from books and articles to blogs and social media posts, and seeking out diverse voices and viewpoints.

❖ **Learn from others:** Learning from others is a great way to expand your knowledge and skills. This means seeking out mentors and advisors, as well as networking with others in your field or industry.

By embracing curiosity, seeking out new experiences, investing in education, reading widely, and learning from others, you can cultivate a commitment to continuous learning and stay competitive in an ever-changing world.

Financial literacy: Finally, financial literacy is a key element of the mindset required for making money. Understanding the basics of personal finance, such as budgeting, saving, investing, and debt management, is essential for making informed financial decisions. Financial literacy is an important component of the mindset required for making money. It refers to the knowledge and skills necessary to make informed decisions about managing money, including budgeting, saving, investing, and managing debt. Building financial literacy can help you make better financial decisions and build wealth over time.

Here are some ways to cultivate financial literacy:

❖ **Start with the basics:** Building financial literacy starts with understanding the basics of personal finance. This means learning about topics like budgeting, saving, and managing debt, as well as understanding financial terms and concepts.

❖ **Learn from experts:** Learning from financial experts can be a great way to build your financial literacy. This means seeking out books, courses, and other resources from trusted financial experts and advisors.

- ❖ **Stay up-to-date:** Staying up-to-date on financial news and trends is important for building financial literacy. This means staying informed about market trends, economic indicators, and other factors that can impact your finances.

- ❖ **Practice good financial habits:** Practicing good financial habits is an important part of building financial literacy. This means living within your means, paying bills on time, and saving for the future.

- ❖ **Seek out professional advice:** Seeking out professional advice can be a great way to build your financial literacy. This means working with a financial advisor or planner who can help you make informed decisions about managing your money.

By starting with the basics, learning from experts, staying up-to-date, practicing good financial habits, and seeking out professional advice, you can build your financial literacy and make informed decisions about managing your money.

In conclusion, the mindset required for making money is about having a positive attitude, being creative and resourceful, taking calculated risks, being persistent and resilient, continuously learning, and having financial literacy. By adopting this mindset, you can create the foundation for financial success and achieve your goals.

IMPORTANCE OF FINANCIAL LITERACY

Financial literacy is important for several reasons:

- ❖ **Making informed financial decisions:** When you have financial literacy, you can make informed financial decisions. This means you can evaluate financial products and services, choose the ones that fit your needs, and avoid costly mistakes.

- ❖ **Building wealth:** Financial literacy helps you build wealth by making it easier to save, invest, and grow your money. When you understand how money works and how to manage it effectively, you can make your money work for you.

- ❖ **Avoiding debt and financial problems:** Financial literacy can help you avoid debt and financial problems. When you understand how to budget, save, and manage debt, you can avoid falling into financial traps that can lead to long-term financial problems.

- ❖ **Achieving financial goals:** Financial literacy is essential for achieving financial goals, whether that's buying a house, starting a business, or retiring comfortably. When you understand how to manage your money effectively, you can create a plan that helps you achieve your financial goals.

- ❖ **Protecting yourself and your family:** Financial literacy can also help you protect yourself and your family. When you understand how to manage your money, you can make sure that you have enough money set aside for emergencies, and that your family is financially protected in the event of a crisis.

DEFINING GOALS AND CREATING A PLAN

Defining goals and creating a plan is an important step in making money. This involves setting clear financial goals and developing a plan to achieve them. Here are some steps to follow:

- ❖ **Define your financial goals:** To make money, it's important to have clear financial goals. This means defining what you want to achieve, such as buying a house, starting a business, or retiring comfortably. It's important to be specific and realistic when setting your goals.

❖ **Create a plan:** Once you've defined your financial goals, the next step is to create a plan to achieve them. This means breaking down your goals into smaller, more manageable steps. For example, if your goal is to start a business, your plan might include researching your market, developing a business plan, and securing funding.

❖ **Determine your timeline:** It's important to have a timeline for achieving your financial goals. This means setting deadlines for each step in your plan and tracking your progress along the way. It's important to be realistic about how long each step will take.

❖ **Make adjustments as needed:** It's important to be flexible when working toward your financial goals. This means being willing to make adjustments to your plan as needed. For example, if you encounter unexpected challenges or opportunities, you may need to adjust your timeline or your approach to achieving your goals.

❖ **Monitor your progress:** To stay on track with your financial goals, it's important to monitor your progress regularly. This means tracking your income, expenses, and savings, and making adjustments as needed to stay on track.

CHAPTER 2

STARTING A BUSINESS

Starting a business is one way to make money, but it requires careful planning and preparation. Starting a business can be a rewarding and challenging experience. Here are some steps to consider when starting a business:

- **Identify your niche:** The first step in starting a business is identifying your niche. This means finding a gap in the market and developing a product or service that meets a specific need.

- **Conduct market research:** Before launching your business, it's important to conduct market research. This means analyzing the market and your competition to determine demand for your product or service and identify potential customers.

- ❖ **Develop a business plan:** A business plan is a roadmap for your business. It should include a description of your business, your target market, your competition, your marketing strategy, and your financial projections.

- ❖ **Secure funding:** Starting a business requires funding. This means finding investors, securing a loan, or using personal savings to finance your business.

- ❖ **Register your business:** Before launching your business, it's important to register it with the appropriate authorities. This may include registering your business name, obtaining business licenses and permits, and registering for taxes.

- ❖ **Build your team:** As your business grows, you may need to build a team of employees or contractors. This means recruiting, hiring, and training the right people to help you achieve your business goals.

❖ **Launch your business:** Once you've completed all of the necessary preparations, it's time to launch your business. This means promoting your product or service, building your customer base, and growing your business over time.

IDENTIFYING YOUR PASSION AND TURNING IT INTO A PROFITABLE VENTURE

Identifying your passion and turning it into a profitable venture is a common approach that many successful entrepreneurs have taken. Here are some steps you can take to identify your passion and turn it into a profitable business:

❖ **Identify your interests and skills:** Take time to think about the things that you enjoy doing and are good at. This could be a hobby, a talent, or a skill that you have developed over time. Make a list of these interests and skills to get a clearer picture of what you could potentially turn into a business.

❖ **Research the market:** Once you have identified your interests and skills, research the market to see if there is a demand for what you want to offer. Look for gaps or niches in the market that you can fill with your passion. Consider conducting surveys, focus groups, or speaking with potential customers to gain a better understanding of what they need and how your passion can meet those needs.

❖ **Develop a business plan:** A business plan is essential for turning your passion into a profitable venture. It will help you outline your goals, target market, financial projections, marketing strategies, and operational plans. A business plan will also help you identify potential challenges and develop contingency plans to overcome them.

❖ **Test your idea:** Before launching your business, test your idea to see if it will work. This could involve creating a prototype, offering a small-scale version of your product or service, or conducting a soft launch to gauge interest and gather feedback from customers.

- **Build a team:** As your business grows, you will likely need to build a team to help you manage the workload. Identify the skills and experience you need and look for people who share your passion and vision for the business.

- **Stay flexible and adaptable:** Building a profitable business from your passion requires flexibility and adaptability. Be open to change and willing to adjust your plans as needed to stay competitive and meet the needs of your customers.

In conclusion, identifying your passion and turning it into a profitable venture requires careful planning, research, and execution. By identifying your interests and skills, researching the market, developing a business plan, testing your idea, building a team, and staying flexible and adaptable, you can increase your chances of success and achieve your financial goals while doing something you love.

CREATING A BUSINESS PLAN AND MARKET RESEARCH

Creating a business plan is an important step towards starting and running a successful business. Here are the key elements to consider when creating a business plan:

- ❖ **Executive Summary:**
  This is a brief overview of your business and should include the purpose, goals, and key features of your business. It should be concise and engaging, capturing the reader's attention and motivating them to read on.

- ❖ **Company Description:**
  This section provides a more detailed description of your business, including its history, legal structure, and location. It should also describe the products or

services you offer and how they meet the needs of your target market.

❖ **Market Analysis:**
This section outlines the market size, trends, and competition in your industry. It also identifies your target customers and their needs. You should conduct thorough research to gather data about your target market and competition.

❖ **Products and Services:**
This section describes your products and services in detail and how they meet the needs of your target customers. You should explain the benefits and unique selling points of your products or services, and how they compare to those of your competitors.

❖ **Marketing and Sales:**
This section outlines your marketing strategies and sales plan to reach your target customers. It should describe how you will promote your business, how you will reach

your target audience, and how you will measure the success of your marketing efforts.

- ❖ **Financial Projections:**
  This section includes financial statements such as cash flow statements, income statements, and balance sheets, as well as projected revenue and expenses. You should also include your funding requirements, how you plan to use the funds, and how you plan to repay any loans or investments.

- ❖ **Implementation and Timeline:**
  This section outlines the steps you need to take to implement your business plan, including the resources you need and the timeline for each step. It should also identify any risks or challenges that you may face and how you plan to mitigate them.

  When creating your business plan, make sure it is well-organized, easy to read, and contains accurate and up-to-date information. You may want to seek input from others, such as mentors or business advisors, to help you refine your plan and ensure its success.

MARKET RESEARCH

Market research is the process of gathering and analyzing information about your target market, competitors, and industry trends. It helps you to understand your customers' needs and preferences, identify your competition, and make informed decisions about your business.

Here are some steps to conduct market research:

❖ **Define your target market:** Identify the characteristics of your ideal customer such as age, gender, location, and buying habits.

❖ **Analyze your competition:** Research your competitors' products or services, prices, and marketing strategies.

❖ **Conduct surveys or focus groups:** Gather feedback from potential customers to identify their needs, preferences, and opinions about your product or service.

❖ **Analyze industry trends:** Stay up-to-date with industry news, trends, and regulations that may affect your business.

❖ **Use online tools:** Utilize online tools such as Google Analytics, social media insights, and keyword research to gather data about your target market.

Creating a business plan and conducting market research are essential steps to starting and growing a successful business. A well-crafted business plan will help you to stay focused on your objectives, while market research will provide valuable insights into your target market, competition, and industry trends. Together, these steps will help you to make informed decisions and increase your chances of success.

UNDERSTANDING THE LEGAL AND FINANCIAL ASPECTS OF STARTING A BUSINESS

Understanding the legal and financial aspects of starting a business is crucial to ensuring its success. Here are some key considerations to keep in mind:

- ❖ **Legal structure:** You will need to choose a legal structure for your business, such as a sole proprietorship, partnership, limited liability company (LLC), or corporation. Each structure has its own advantages and disadvantages in terms of liability, taxation, and management.

❖ **Permits and licenses:** Depending on the type of business you are starting, you may need to obtain permits and licenses from local, state, or federal government agencies. This may include zoning permits, health permits, and business licenses.

❖ **Taxes:** As a business owner, you will be responsible for paying various taxes, such as income tax, self-employment tax, and sales tax. It's important to understand your tax obligations and to keep accurate records of all business expenses and income.

❖ **Insurance:** Depending on the nature of your business, you may need to obtain various types of insurance, such as liability insurance, property insurance, and workers' compensation insurance.

Insurance can help protect your business from unexpected events and liabilities.

❖ **Contracts and agreements:** As a business owner, you will likely need to enter into various contracts and agreements with suppliers, customers, employees, and other stakeholders. It's important to have a basic understanding of contract law and to consult with an attorney when necessary.

❖ **Financing:** Starting a business can be expensive, and you may need to obtain financing from investors, lenders, or other sources. It's important to understand the different types of financing available and to have a solid understanding of your business's financial needs and projections.

❖ **Accounting and bookkeeping:** Keeping accurate financial records is essential for any business. It's important to understand basic accounting and bookkeeping principles and to use accounting software or hire a professional accountant to help manage your finances.

Understanding the legal and financial aspects of starting a business is essential to ensuring its success. By choosing the right legal structure, obtaining the necessary permits and licenses, understanding your tax obligations, obtaining insurance, entering into contracts and agreements, securing financing, and keeping accurate financial records, you can increase your chances of success and achieve your financial goals. It's important to consult with professionals such as attorneys, accountants, and financial advisors when necessary to ensure that you are making informed decisions and complying with all legal and financial requirements.

CHAPTER 3

INVESTING IN STOCKS AND SHARES

Investing in stocks and shares can be an excellent way to grow your wealth over the long term. Here are some key elements to consider when investing in stocks and shares:

Choose the Right Investment Platform:

There are various investment platforms available, including traditional brokerage firms, online brokers, and robo-advisors. Choose a platform that aligns with your investment goals, risk tolerance, and budget.

Conduct Thorough Research:
Before investing in a stock or share, conduct thorough research on the company, industry, and market trends. Analyze the company's financial statements, management team, and competitive landscape to determine its potential for growth.

Diversify Your Portfolio:
Diversification is crucial to manage risk and minimize potential losses. Spread your investments across different companies, sectors, and asset classes to minimize the impact of a single company's poor performance.

Understand Risk:
Investing in stocks and shares carries risks, including market volatility, company-

specific risks, and macroeconomic risks. It's important to understand these risks and manage them through diversification, asset allocation, and risk management techniques.

Invest for the Long Term:
Investing in stocks and shares requires patience and a long-term perspective. It's essential to stay focused on your investment goals and avoid making hasty decisions based on short-term market fluctuations.

Choose the Right Investment Strategy:
There are various investment strategies available, including value investing, growth investing, and income investing. Choose a strategy that aligns with your investment goals, risk tolerance, and time horizon.

Monitor Your Investments:
Regularly monitor your investments and make adjustments as needed. Stay informed about market trends and economic

developments that could impact your investments.

Seek Professional Advice:
If you're unsure about how to invest in stocks and shares, seek professional advice from a financial advisor or investment professional. They can provide guidance on investment strategies, risk management, and portfolio diversification.

Investing in stocks and shares can be an excellent way to grow your wealth over the long term, but it's essential to conduct thorough research, understand risk, and choose the right investment strategy. Stay focused on your investment goals and seek professional advice as needed

UNDERSTANDING THE STOCK MARKET AND HOW IT WORKS

The stock market is a complex system of buying and selling stocks (also known as shares or equities) in companies that are publicly listed. There are some key elements to understanding the stock market:

Stock Market Participants:
The stock market has various participants, including individual investors, institutional

investors (such as mutual funds or pension funds), traders, and market makers. Each participant has a different role in the market.

Stock Exchange:
The stock market operates through stock exchanges, which are platforms where buyers and sellers meet to trade shares. The most well-known exchanges are the New York Stock Exchange (NYSE) and NASDAQ.

Stock Prices:
Stock prices fluctuate based on supply and demand. When there is high demand for a stock, the price goes up, and when there is low demand, the price goes down.

Stock Indices:
Stock indices, such as the S&P 500 or the Dow Jones Industrial Average, are used to track the overall performance of the stock market. They are a weighted average of the

prices of selected stocks and are used as benchmarks for investors.

Fundamental Analysis:
Fundamental analysis is a method used to evaluate the financial health of a company and its future growth prospects. It involves analyzing financial statements, industry trends, and other macroeconomic factors to determine the value of a company's stock.

Technical Analysis:
Technical analysis is a method used to analyze stock price movements and identify patterns to make trading decisions. It involves using charts and technical indicators to predict future price movements.

Trading Strategies:
There are various trading strategies used by investors, including value investing, growth investing, and day trading. Each strategy has its advantages and disadvantages, and it's essential to understand them before investing.

Let's take a quick look at the investment strategies mentioned above

❖ **Growth investing** is an investment strategy that focuses on investing in companies that are expected to experience significant growth in the future. The goal is to identify companies that have the potential to generate higher-than-average returns and hold them for the long term.

Here are some tips to consider in growth investing:

Invest in High-Growth Companies:
Growth investors look for companies with high growth potential, such as companies in emerging industries or those with innovative products or services. These companies typically have a higher price-to-earnings ratio (P/E ratio) than the market average.

Focus on Earnings Growth:

Growth investors pay close attention to a company's earnings growth rate, as this is a key indicator of future growth potential. They look for companies with consistent and accelerating earnings growth.

Consider Market Trends:
Growth investors also consider market trends and shifts in consumer behavior when identifying potential growth companies. They look for companies that are well-positioned to capitalize on these trends and have a competitive advantage over their competitors.

Invest for the Long Term:
Growth investing is a long-term strategy, and growth investors often hold their investments for years, if not decades. This approach allows the company to continue growing and the stock price to increase over time.

Diversify Your Portfolio:

Like all investment strategies, growth investing involves risk, and it's important to diversify your portfolio to minimize risk. Growth investors typically invest in a portfolio of growth stocks across various industries and sectors.

Growth investing can be a successful investment strategy for those willing to take on a higher level of risk and invest for the long term. However, it's important to remember that all investing involves risk, and past performance is no guarantee of future results. It's important to conduct thorough research, analyze fundamentals, and diversify your portfolio to minimize risk.

❖ **Value investing** is an investment strategy that involves identifying undervalued companies whose stocks are trading below their intrinsic value. This strategy was popularized by Benjamin Graham and David Dodd in their book "Security Analysis" and further refined by Warren Buffett.

Here are some key factors to consider in value investing:

Focus on Intrinsic Value:
Value investors believe that the market can sometimes misprice stocks, resulting in a gap between a company's stock price and its intrinsic value. The goal is to identify these undervalued stocks and buy them at a discount.

Look for Margin of Safety:
Value investors also seek a margin of safety by buying stocks at a price significantly below their intrinsic value. This approach helps to minimize downside risk if the stock price drops.

Analyze Fundamentals:
Value investors analyze a company's fundamental metrics such as earnings, cash flow, book value, and dividends to determine its intrinsic value. They compare these metrics with industry averages and historical trends to identify undervalued stocks.

Invest for the Long Term:
Value investing is a long-term strategy, and value investors often hold stocks for years, if not decades. This approach allows the market to recognize the company's true value and for the stock price to rise over time.

Focus on Quality:
Value investors also look for high-quality companies with strong competitive advantages, stable earnings, and a proven track record of success. These factors reduce the risk of investing in undervalued companies.

Be Patient:
Value investing requires patience and discipline. Value investors may need to wait for a long time for the market to recognize the company's true value and for the stock

price to rise. However, patience can result in significant returns over the long term.

Value investing can be a successful investment strategy for those willing to put in the time and effort to conduct thorough research, analyze fundamentals, and invest for the long term. However, it's important to remember that all investing involves risk and to diversify your portfolio to minimize risk.

❖ **Income investing** is an investment strategy that focuses on generating a steady stream of income from investments. This strategy is often used by investors who are nearing retirement or looking for a steady income stream to supplement their regular income.

Here are some key tips for income investing:

Invest in Income-Producing Assets:
Income investors typically invest in assets that produce income, such as bonds, dividend-paying stocks, and real estate

investment trusts (REITs). These assets typically provide a regular stream of income in the form of interest, dividends, or rental income.

Focus on Yield:
Yield is a measure of the income generated by an investment, usually expressed as a percentage of the investment's value. Income investors focus on the yield of their investments, seeking out assets with a high yield relative to their risk level.

Look for Stability:
Income investors also prioritize stability in their investments. They seek out assets with a steady income stream and a low risk of default or volatility. This may include investments in established companies with a history of consistent dividends or high-quality bonds.

Consider Tax Implications:
Income investors also pay close attention to the tax implications of their investments. For example, they may choose to invest in

municipal bonds, which are typically exempt from federal income tax and may be exempt from state and local taxes as well.

Diversify Your Portfolio:
Like all investment strategies, income investing involves risk, and it's important to diversify your portfolio to minimize risk. Income investors typically invest in a portfolio of income-producing assets across various industries and sectors.

Income investing can be a successful investment strategy for those looking for a steady income stream from their investments. However, it's important to remember that all investing involves risk, and past performance is no guarantee of future results. It's important to conduct thorough research, analyze fundamentals, and diversify your portfolio to minimize risk. Additionally, income investing may not be suitable for all investors, depending on their individual financial goals and risk tolerance.

Overall, understanding the stock market and how it works is essential for investors who want to make informed investment decisions. It's important to conduct thorough research and seek professional advice before investing in the stock market.

LEARNING HOW TO ANALYZE STOCKS AND MAKE INFORMED DECISIONS

Learning how to analyze stocks and make informed investment decisions is essential for anyone looking to invest in the stock market.

Here are some key principles of stock analysis:

Fundamental Analysis:
Fundamental analysis involves examining a company's financial health, industry trends, and economic conditions to evaluate the potential of its stock. Key factors to consider include earnings growth, revenue growth, profit margins, and debt levels.

Technical Analysis:
Technical analysis involves using charts and statistical analysis to identify trends and patterns in a stock's price and volume. Key indicators to consider include moving averages, relative strength index (RSI), and Bollinger Bands.

Valuation:
Valuation is the process of determining the intrinsic value of a stock. This involves

comparing the stock's price to its earnings, cash flow, and book value. Key valuation metrics to consider include the price-to-earnings ratio (P/E ratio), price-to-book ratio (P/B ratio), and price-to-sales ratio (P/S ratio).

Market Analysis:
Market analysis involves examining broader economic and market trends to identify potential opportunities and risks. Key factors to consider include interest rates, inflation, and geopolitical events.

Risk Management:
Effective risk management is essential to successful investing. This involves setting investment goals, diversifying your portfolio, and managing your exposure to risk through strategies such as stop-loss orders and position sizing.

Keep up with news and events:
Staying up to date with news and events related to the company or industry is

essential in making informed investment decisions. This could include announcements related to earnings, product launches, mergers and acquisitions, or regulatory changes.

It's Important to note that there is no one-size-fits-all approach to stock analysis, and different investors may prioritize different factors based on their investment goals and risk tolerance. It's also important to conduct thorough research and consult with a financial professional before making any investment decisions.

THE RISKS AND REWARDS OF INVESTING IN STOCKS

Investing in stocks can offer both rewards and risks. There are two key considerations to keep in mind before investing in the stock market. The Rewards, The risks.

Rewards

Potential for High Returns:
Stocks have the potential to offer higher returns than other investment options over the long-term, although this also comes with greater risks.

Diversification:
Investing in a range of stocks can offer diversification benefits, which can help spread risk and reduce overall portfolio volatility.

Ownership:
By investing in stocks, you own a piece of the company and can potentially benefit from its success through share price appreciation and dividends.

Inflation Hedge:
Stocks can offer a hedge against inflation as companies can pass on rising costs to consumers through higher prices, which can help maintain profitability and stock prices.

Risks:

Volatility:
Stock prices can be volatile and can experience significant fluctuations in response to economic, political, or industry-specific events.

Loss of Capital:
Investing in stocks comes with the risk of losing money, as stock prices can decline, sometimes significantly and quickly.

Market Risk:
The stock market as a whole can be impacted by broader economic and political events, such as recessions, inflation, and

interest rate changes, which can lead to market-wide declines.

Company Risk:
Individual companies can face risks, such as increased competition, changes in consumer preferences, or regulatory changes, which can negatively impact their stock price.

Liquidity Risk:
Investing in less liquid stocks can make it harder to sell shares quickly, which can be problematic if you need to raise cash quickly.

It's important to note that investing in stocks carries risks and rewards, and it's important to carefully consider your investment goals, risk tolerance, and time horizon before making any investment decisions. It's also a good idea to consult with a financial professional to help ensure that your investment strategy aligns with your goals and risk tolerance.

CHAPTER 4

Investing in Real Estate

Real estate refers to land, buildings, and other physical properties, including natural resources such as minerals, water, and crops, as well as any rights and interests associated with them. Real estate can be used for residential, commercial, industrial, or agricultural purposes.

In addition to the physical properties themselves, real estate also includes the legal and financial aspects associated with buying, selling, and managing properties. This includes the processes involved in property ownership, such as property taxes, insurance, and maintenance.

Real estate is a key component of the economy, as it provides housing and other essential services, as well as employment opportunities in construction, real estate management, and related industries. Additionally, real estate is often considered a valuable investment, as it can appreciate in value over time and provide income through

rental properties or capital gains from property sales.
Investing in real estate can offer several potential benefits, including:

Cash Flow:
Real estate can generate rental income, which can provide a steady stream of cash flow for investors.

Appreciation:
Real estate can also appreciate in value over time, which can lead to capital gains for investors if they sell the property at a higher price than they bought it.

Inflation Hedge:
Real estate can provide a hedge against inflation, as rental income and property values tend to rise in tandem with inflation.

Tax Benefits:

Real estate investors can benefit from tax deductions, such as mortgage interest, property taxes, and depreciation.
There are different ways to invest in real estate, some of these are:

Direct Ownership:
Investors can purchase a property outright and manage it themselves, or hire a property manager to handle day-to-day operations.

Real Estate Investment Trusts (REITs):
REITs are companies that own, operate, or finance income-producing real estate properties. Investors can buy shares of a publicly-traded REIT, which can provide exposure to real estate without the hassle of direct ownership.

Real Estate Crowdfunding:
Investors can also participate in real estate crowdfunding, which allows multiple investors to pool their money together to invest in a real estate project.

However, there are also potential risks to investing in real estate, including:

Market Risk:
Real estate values can fluctuate based on economic conditions, such as interest rates, unemployment rates, and supply and demand.

Property-Specific Risks:
Individual properties can face risks, such as natural disasters, tenant defaults, and property damage, which can negatively impact their value and cash flow.

Liquidity Risk:
Real estate investments can be illiquid, meaning it can be difficult to sell the property quickly if needed.

Regulatory Risks:
Real estate investors also need to be aware of regulations and laws that may impact their investments, such as zoning laws, building codes, and tax laws.

As with any investment, it's important to carefully consider your investment goals, risk tolerance, and time horizon before investing in real estate. It's also a good idea to consult with a financial professional to help ensure that your investment strategy aligns with your goals and risk tolerance.

UNDERSTANDING THE REAL ESTATE MARKET AND IT'S POTENTIAL PROFIT

Understanding the real estate market is an essential aspect of investing in real estate and realizing its potential for profit. The real estate market is dynamic and can be influenced by a range of factors, including the local and national economy, demographics, interest rates, and supply and demand.

One way to assess the real estate market is by looking at market trends, such as average home prices, the number of homes for sale, and the length of time homes remain on the market. Market trends can give investors insights into the direction of the market and help them make informed decisions about when and where to invest.

Another important consideration when investing in real estate is the potential for profit. Real estate can be a valuable investment because it offers a range of income streams, including rental income, capital gains, and tax benefits.

Rental income is generated by renting out a property to tenants, and it can provide a steady income stream for investors. Capital gains are realized when a property is sold for more than its purchase price, and they can be a significant source of profit for investors who purchase undervalued properties and sell them for a higher price. Additionally, real estate investments can offer tax benefits, such as deductions for mortgage interest and property taxes.

However, it is important to remember that investing in real estate also comes with risks, such as fluctuations in the real estate market, unexpected expenses, and the potential for vacancies and unpaid rent. To mitigate these risks, investors should conduct thorough market research, develop a solid financial plan, and consider working with a professional real estate agent or property management company.

TYPES OF REAL ESTATE INVESTMENT, THEIR ADVANTAGES AND DISADVANTAGES

There are several types of real estate investments that investors can consider, each with its own advantages and disadvantages. Here are some of the most common types:

Residential Real Estate: This type of real estate includes single-family homes, condos, townhouses, and multi-family properties. The advantages of investing in residential real estate are that it can offer a steady income stream through rental income and long-term appreciation, as well as tax benefits. However, the disadvantages are that it can require a significant initial investment, and there is a risk of vacancies and tenant turnover.

Commercial Real Estate: This type of real estate includes office buildings, retail space, industrial properties, and hotels. The advantages of investing in commercial real estate are that it can offer higher returns than residential real estate, longer lease terms, and stable cash flow. However, the disadvantages are that it can require a larger initial investment and may be more complex to manage than residential properties.

Real Estate Investment Trusts (REITs): REITs are companies that own and manage real estate properties and allow investors to invest in a diversified portfolio of properties. The advantages of investing in REITs are that they offer a low-cost and easy way to invest in real estate, provide regular income through dividends, and offer liquidity. However, the disadvantages are that investors have no control over the management of the properties and may be subject to market fluctuations.

Real Estate Crowdfunding: This is a newer type of real estate investment that allows investors to pool their money together to invest in a specific property or portfolio of properties. The advantages of investing in real estate crowdfunding are that it can offer lower minimum investments, higher returns than traditional investments, and allow investors to diversify their portfolio. However, the disadvantages are that it is a relatively new and untested investment type, and investors may be subject to high fees.

Real Estate Partnerships: This type of investment involves forming a partnership with other investors to purchase and manage a property. The advantages of investing in real estate partnerships are that it can offer the opportunity to invest in larger properties with a lower initial investment and allow investors to share the responsibilities of property management. However, the disadvantages are that it can be challenging to find trustworthy partners, and investors may be subject to disagreements and conflicts.

When considering a real estate investment, it is essential to conduct thorough research and analysis to determine which type of investment best fits your goals and risk tolerance. Additionally, it is essential to work with a reputable and experienced real estate agent or financial advisor to ensure that you are making informed investment decisions.

FINANCING OPTIONS AND PROPERTY MANAGEMENT

When it comes to investing in real estate, there are several financing options available, including traditional mortgages, hard money loans, and private money loans.

Traditional mortgages are loans obtained through banks or other lending institutions, and they typically require a significant down payment, good credit, and a solid income history. These loans can be used to purchase residential or commercial properties, and they typically offer relatively low interest rates and longer repayment terms.

Hard money loans are a type of short-term, high-interest loan that is often used for real estate investments. These loans are typically obtained through private investors or companies, and they are secured by the property being purchased. Hard money loans can be a good option for investors who need quick access to cash or who have poor credit, but they typically come with higher interest rates and shorter repayment terms than traditional mortgages.

Private money loans are another financing option that involves borrowing money from individuals or companies rather than traditional lending institutions. These loans can be used for a variety of real estate investments and typically come with more flexible terms than traditional mortgages, but they may also come with higher interest rates.

In addition to financing options, property management is another key aspect of real estate investing. Property management involves the day-to-day operations of managing a property, including rent collection, maintenance and repairs, and tenant screening. Property management can be done by the property owner or by a professional property management company. Effective property management is crucial for maintaining the value of the property and maximizing its income potential.

CHAPTER 5

Freelancing and Consulting

Freelancing and consulting are two popular ways to make money in today's gig economy. Both involve providing services to clients on a project-by-project basis, rather than being employed by a company on a full-time basis.

Freelancing:

Freelancing is essentially self-employment, where you offer your skills or expertise to clients as a contractor. Freelancers typically work remotely and may specialize in a variety of areas, including writing, graphic design, programming, web development, social media management, and more.

❖ **Advantages of freelancing**

Flexibility: Freelancers have the freedom to choose their own projects, set their own schedule, and work from anywhere.

Potential for higher earnings: As a freelancer, you can set your own rates and negotiate with clients directly, potentially earning more than you would in a traditional salaried position.

Variety of projects: As a freelancer, you may work on a variety of projects for different clients, which can help you develop new skills and broaden your experience.

❖ **Disadvantages of freelancing**

Inconsistent income: Freelancers may experience peaks and valleys in their income, depending on the volume of work and the clients they have.

No benefits: Freelancers are responsible for their own benefits, such as health insurance and retirement savings.

Self-promotion: As a freelancer, you will need to market yourself and actively seek out new clients to keep a steady stream of work.

Consulting:
Consulting involves providing specialized expertise and advice to clients on a specific topic or issue. Consultants may work independently or as part of a consulting firm, and their clients can be in a wide range of industries.

❖ **Advantages of consulting**
High earning potential: Experienced consultants can command high fees for their services, especially in specialized areas such as management consulting or legal consulting.

Flexibility: Consultants have the ability to work remotely and may be able to choose their own projects and clients.

Variety of projects: Like freelancers, consultants may work on a variety of projects for different clients, which can help them develop new skills and broaden their experience.

❖ **Disadvantages of consulting include:**

Intense competition: The consulting industry is highly competitive, with many experienced professionals vying for the same clients.

No guarantee of steady work: Like freelancers, consultants may experience fluctuations in their workload and income.

Requires specialized expertise: To succeed as a consultant, you need to have a deep understanding of a specific area and be able to provide valuable insights and advice to clients.

IDENTIFYING YOUR SKILLS AND MARKETABLE SERVICES

Identifying your skills and marketable services is crucial in freelancing and consulting as it helps you to position yourself in the market and attract potential clients. Here are simple ways to identify your skills and marketable services:

Identify your strengths and expertise: Start by making a list of your skills, experience, and expertise. This could include anything from writing and editing to graphic design or social media management. Be honest with yourself about what you're good at and what you enjoy doing.

Research the market: Once you've identified your strengths, research the market to see what services are in demand. Look for gaps in the market that you could fill with your skills and expertise. This could involve targeting a niche market or offering a unique service that sets you apart from your competitors.

Define your target audience: Knowing your target audience is crucial in marketing your services effectively. Think about who would benefit from your services and what problems you could solve for them. This could involve targeting specific industries or businesses of a certain size.

Develop a value proposition: Your value proposition is a statement that outlines what makes you unique and why clients should choose to work with you. It should be clear, concise, and focused on the benefits that you offer.

Set your rates: Once you've identified your skills and marketable services, research the market to see what similar freelancers or consultants are charging. Be realistic about your rates, but also factor in your experience, expertise, and the value you bring to the table.

Build your portfolio: Having a portfolio of your work is essential in showcasing your skills and expertise to potential clients. Include case studies, testimonials, and examples of your work that demonstrate your abilities and the value you bring to your clients.

Market your services: Finally, marketing your services effectively is crucial in attracting clients. Use social media, networking events, and online marketplaces to promote your services and build your brand. Develop a marketing strategy that targets your ideal clients and showcases your skills and expertise.

BUILDING A CLIENT BASE AND SETTING RATES

Building a client base and setting rates are two important aspects of starting a successful freelancing or consulting business.

Building a client base
- One of the biggest challenges in freelancing and consulting is finding clients. To build a client base, consider the following tips:
- Develop a strong online presence through social media, a professional website, and online directories.
- Use job boards and freelancer platforms to find short-term and long-term projects.
- Attend networking events and conferences to meet potential clients in person.

- Ask for referrals from satisfied clients.
- Offer a free consultation or trial service to attract potential clients.

Setting rates
- Setting rates can be tricky, as you want to be competitive while still valuing your time and expertise. Here are some tips:
- Research the market to see what other freelancers and consultants charge for similar services.
- Consider your experience, education, and specialized skills when setting your rates.
- Factor in any overhead costs, such as software subscriptions, equipment, and office space.
- Offer different pricing packages, such as hourly rates, flat project fees, or retainer agreements.
- Be transparent with clients about your rates and billing policies.

By building a strong client base and setting competitive rates, you can establish yourself as a successful freelancer or consultant in your field.

MARKETING YOUR SERVICES EFFECTIVELY

Marketing your services effectively is crucial to attracting and retaining clients as a freelancer or consultant. Here are some tips on how to market your services effectively:

Develop a marketing strategy:
Before you start marketing your services, develop a strategy that outlines your goals, target audience, message, and marketing channels. This will help you stay focused and make the most of your marketing efforts.

Create a strong brand:

Your brand is how clients perceive you and your services. To create a strong brand, consider the following:
- Develop a unique value proposition that sets you apart from your competition.
- Choose a memorable name and logo that reflects your brand identity.
- Use consistent branding across all marketing channels, including your website, social media, and business cards.
- Leverage social media:
- Social media is a powerful tool for promoting your services and building relationships with clients. Consider the following tips:
- Choose the social media platforms that your target audience uses the most.
- Post engaging content regularly, such as articles, tips, and industry news.
- Engage with your followers by responding to comments and messages.
- Use paid social media ads to target potential clients.

Network in-person:

While online marketing is important, in-person networking can also be valuable. Attend conferences, trade shows, and networking events to meet potential clients and build relationships with industry professionals.

Offer incentives:

Offering incentives can be a great way to attract new clients and retain existing ones. Consider offering discounts for referrals or providing free consultations to new clients.

By developing a marketing strategy, creating a strong brand, leveraging social media, networking in-person, and offering incentives, you can effectively market your services and attract more clients as a freelancer or consultant.

CHAPTER 6

ONLINE BUSINESS AND E-COMMERCE

Online business and e-commerce are rapidly growing industries with limitless potential for individuals looking to make money. The rise of the internet and the increasing use of technology in daily life has revolutionized the way people conduct business, making it possible for anyone with an internet connection to start and run a successful business.
One of the biggest advantages of starting an online business is the low startup costs. You

don't need to rent a physical space, purchase expensive equipment, or hire employees. With just a laptop and an internet connection, you can create an e-commerce website, blog, or digital product.

When starting an online business, it is essential to identify a marketable product or service. This could be anything from selling physical products, digital products, or offering online services like graphic design, writing, or social media management. It's crucial to do extensive market research to determine if there is a demand for your product or service.

Building a website or online store is a critical step in starting an online business. It's essential to create a user-friendly website that is easy to navigate and visually appealing. You can use platforms like Shopify or WooCommerce to create an online store, and services like WordPress or Squarespace to create a website.

Once you have a website or online store, the next step is to drive traffic to it. This can be done through search engine optimization, social media marketing, email marketing, and pay-per-click advertising. The goal is to generate traffic to your site and convert those visitors into customers.

E-commerce businesses can also leverage platforms like Amazon, Etsy, or eBay to sell their products. These platforms provide a built-in customer base, making it easier to start selling your products quickly.

In conclusion, online business and e-commerce provide a wealth of opportunities for individuals looking to make money. With low startup costs, the potential for high-profit margins, and the ability to work from anywhere in the world, it's no surprise that more people are turning to online business as a viable income stream.

UNDERSTANDING THE POTENTIAL OF ONLINE BUSINESSES AND E-COMMERCE

The potential of online businesses and e-commerce is immense in today's digital age. The internet has provided businesses with an opportunity to reach a global audience and expand their customer base. E-commerce is the buying and selling of products or services over the internet, and online businesses refer to any business that operates primarily online. The benefits of online businesses and e-commerce include lower overhead costs, increased flexibility, and access to a broader customer base.

One significant advantage of an online business is that it is accessible 24/7, providing customers with convenience and flexibility. With an online store, customers can browse and purchase products or services from anywhere in the world at any time, without the need to physically visit a store. This accessibility can lead to increased sales and revenue for the business. E-commerce also provides businesses with the ability to target specific customer demographics through targeted marketing campaigns. By tracking customer behavior and preferences, businesses can tailor their marketing efforts to reach the right audience with the right message, increasing the effectiveness of their advertising.

In addition, online businesses and e-commerce can provide valuable data and insights about customer behavior and preferences. By analyzing data such as website traffic, customer demographics, and purchasing patterns, businesses can make data-driven decisions to improve their products, services, and marketing efforts.

However, like any business venture, online businesses and e-commerce also have their challenges. Competition in the online marketplace can be fierce, and businesses need to differentiate themselves to stand out from the crowd. Building trust with customers can also be a challenge, as many online shoppers are wary of scams and fraudulent websites.

Overall, the potential benefits of online businesses and e-commerce are significant, and with the right strategy and execution, businesses can succeed in the digital marketplace.

CHOOSING THE RIGHT PLATFORM AND CREATING A WEBSITE

Creating an online business or e-commerce site can be a lucrative way to make money, but it can also be challenging to get started. One of the first steps in building an online business is to choose the right platform and create a website.

Choosing the right platform is essential, as it will impact the functionality of your site and the ease with which you can manage and grow your business. There are many e-commerce platforms available, including Shopify, WooCommerce, and BigCommerce. Each platform has its own features and benefits, so it's important to research and compare them to determine which one is the best fit for your business.

Once you've chosen your platform, the next step is to create a website. Your website should be visually appealing, easy to navigate, and provide a clear and concise message about your products or services. It's important to ensure that your website is mobile-friendly, as an increasing number of consumers are shopping and browsing online using their mobile devices.

When creating your website, you should also consider search engine optimization (SEO) to ensure that your site appears at the top of search engine results pages. This involves incorporating relevant keywords, creating high-quality content, and building quality backlinks to your site.

In addition to your website, you may also want to consider selling your products or services on third-party platforms like Amazon or Etsy. These platforms can help you reach a wider audience and can provide additional marketing and promotional opportunities.

Overall, building a successful online business or e-commerce site requires careful planning, attention to detail, and a focus on providing value to your customers. With the right platform, website, and marketing strategies in place, you can create a thriving online business that generates consistent revenue and helps you achieve your financial goals.

MARKETING AND ADVERTISING STRATEGIES

Marketing and advertising strategies are crucial to the success of any online business or e-commerce venture. With the vast competition on the internet, it is essential to stand out from the crowd and get your message across to potential customers.

Here are sure guaranteed ways to get visibility and reach for your online business

Search engine optimization (SEO): SEO involves optimizing your website and content to rank higher in search engine results pages (SERPs). By incorporating relevant keywords, creating high-quality content, and building quality backlinks, you can improve your website's visibility and attract more organic traffic.

Social media marketing: Social media platforms provide an excellent opportunity to connect with your audience and promote your brand. By creating engaging content, responding to comments and messages, and building a strong social media presence, you can attract new customers and increase brand awareness.

Email marketing: Email marketing is an effective way to reach out to potential and existing customers, promote your products or services, and build brand loyalty. By creating targeted email campaigns, you can deliver personalized messages and drive conversions.

Pay-per-click (PPC) advertising: PPC advertising involves paying for clicks on your ads placed on search engine results pages or social media platforms. By targeting the right keywords and demographics, you can attract more relevant traffic to your website and increase conversions but it can also be expensive if not managed properly.

Content marketing: Content marketing involves creating high-quality and valuable content to attract and engage your target audience. By publishing blog posts, videos, infographics, and other types of content, you can build trust, establish your authority in your niche, and attract more leads and customers.

Affiliate marketing: Affiliate marketing involves partnering with other businesses or influencers to promote your products or services in exchange for a commission on sales. By leveraging the reach and influence of your partners, you can expand your customer base and drive sales.

Influencer marketing: Influencer marketing involves partnering with social media influencers who have a large following in your target market. This can be an effective way to reach new customers and build trust and credibility for your brand.

Referral marketing: Referral marketing involves incentivizing your existing customers to refer their friends and family to your business. By offering rewards or discounts, you can motivate your customers to spread the word about your brand and increase your customer base.

CHAPTER 7

CREATING PASSIVE INCOME

Creating passive income is the process of generating income that requires minimal effort to maintain or manage. It is a popular way of making money because it allows you to earn money even while you are not actively working. Creating passive income refers to earning income that requires little to no effort to maintain or continue earning. This type of income can come from various sources such as rental properties, dividends from stocks or mutual funds, royalties from intellectual property, or affiliate marketing. Passive income is a popular method of making money because it allows individuals to earn money without having to actively work for it. However, creating passive income often requires a significant upfront investment of time, money, or both.

One way to create passive income is through rental properties. Real estate investments can generate passive income through rental properties. Property owners can collect rent payments from tenants and use that money to cover expenses, make a profit, or pay off the mortgage. While rental properties can be lucrative, it requires significant initial capital, maintenance, and management.

Investing in dividend-paying stocks or mutual funds is another way to generate passive income. These investments pay out a portion of the company's earnings to shareholders in the form of dividends. Dividend payments can provide a steady stream of income and may increase over time.

Royalties from intellectual property such as patents, trademarks, and copyrights can also generate passive income. For example, an author can earn passive income from book sales, or a musician can earn royalties from their music. If you have created a product or have a patent, you can earn royalties from the sales or licensing of your product.

Affiliate marketing is another way to generate passive income. This involves promoting other people's products or services through an affiliate link. When someone clicks on the link and makes a purchase, the affiliate earns a commission.

Peer-to-peer lending: Peer-to-peer lending involves lending money to individuals or businesses through online platforms. You can earn interest on the loans you make, generating passive income.

Investing in a business: You can invest in a business and receive a share of the profits without having to actively participate in running the business.

It is important to note that creating passive income requires effort and work upfront. However, once you have established a passive income stream, it can provide financial security and freedom. Creating passive income involves finding ways to earn money that require little to no effort to maintain. While it can provide a steady stream of income, it often requires significant upfront investment and careful planning.

UNDERSTANDING WHAT PASSIVE INCOME IS AND HOW IT WORKS

Passive income is income that is earned without the need for active involvement or effort from the recipient. Unlike traditional forms of income that require constant effort, such as a job or running a business, passive income can be generated through various channels such as rental income, investments, and royalties.

Passive income can provide a sense of financial security and freedom as it allows individuals to earn money without having to actively work for it. This means that they can enjoy their time pursuing other passions, hobbies, or even generating additional streams of passive income.

Some common examples of passive income include rental income from properties, dividends from stocks and mutual funds, interest from bank accounts, royalties from intellectual property such as books or music, and income from affiliate marketing or online courses.

To generate passive income, it is important to identify a reliable and sustainable source of income that requires minimal effort to maintain. This may involve investing in assets that appreciate in value over time, or creating a passive income stream through online platforms or businesses that generate recurring revenue.

It is also important to understand the tax implications of passive income and how to effectively manage and invest earnings for long-term growth.

CREATING INCOME STREAMS THROUGH INVESTMENT AND RENTAL PROPERTIES

Creating passive income streams through investments and rental properties can be an effective way to generate consistent income without actively working. Passive income is income that requires little to no effort to maintain and can continue to generate income over time.

One way to create passive income is through investments. Investing in stocks, bonds, mutual funds, or real estate investment trusts (REITs) can generate regular income through dividends, interest payments, or capital gains. Dividend stocks are an excellent way to earn passive income, as

they pay shareholders a portion of the company's profits on a regular basis.
Rental properties are another way to generate passive income. Owning rental properties can provide steady rental income, and the property may also appreciate in value over time. However, it is essential to choose the right property in a desirable location to attract tenants and ensure a steady stream of rental income.

Another way to create passive income is by creating and selling digital products, such as ebooks, courses, or software. Once the product is created, it can continue to generate income without much ongoing effort.

Additionally, investing in a business as a silent partner or investing in a franchise can also generate passive income. The key is to find the right investment that aligns with your interests and financial goals.
It is important to note that creating passive income streams may require an initial

investment of time and money. It is crucial to conduct thorough research and consult with professionals to ensure that the investment is sound and aligns with your financial goals

DEVELOPING AND MARKETING DIGITAL PRODUCTS

Developing and marketing digital products is a growing industry with many opportunities to create passive income. Digital products are items that can be purchased and delivered electronically, such as eBooks, online courses, software, stock photography, graphics, and music.

To create digital products, you need to identify a topic or niche that you have expertise in and can create content around. This can be anything from personal finance to health and wellness to technology. Once you have identified your topic, you can begin creating your content.

One of the benefits of creating digital products is that they can be created once and sold repeatedly, generating passive income. However, it is important to create high-quality content that is valuable to your target audience.

Marketing digital products can be done through various channels, including social media, email marketing, and paid advertising. It is important to identify your target audience and create marketing messages that resonate with them.

Another way to generate passive income through digital products is to use affiliate marketing. This involves promoting other people's products and earning a commission on any sales made through your unique affiliate link.

In addition to creating and marketing digital products, you can also generate passive income through advertising on your website or blog. This can be done through Google AdSense or by selling ad space directly to companies in your niche.

Overall, developing and marketing digital products can be a lucrative way to create passive income, but it requires dedication, expertise, and effective marketing strategies.

CHAPTER 8

Financial Planning and Budgeting

Financial planning and budgeting are critical components of money management, regardless of one's financial situation. Essentially, financial planning involves creating a long-term strategy for achieving your financial goals, while budgeting is about creating a short-term plan for managing your income and expenses. Both of these components are essential for building wealth and achieving financial security.

One of the first steps in financial planning is to identify your long-term financial goals.

This could include things like saving for retirement, paying off debt, or building a college fund for your children. Once you have identified your goals, you can then start to develop a plan for achieving them. This might involve setting aside a portion of your income each month for savings or investment, creating a debt reduction plan, or developing a strategy for increasing your income.

Budgeting is another critical component of financial planning. A budget is essentially a plan for managing your income and expenses on a monthly basis. This might involve tracking your spending, identifying areas where you can cut back on expenses, and creating a plan for paying off debt or building savings. The goal of budgeting is to ensure that you are living within your means and not spending more than you earn.

Another important aspect of financial planning and budgeting is understanding your overall financial situation. This might involve creating a balance sheet that outlines your assets and liabilities, as well as your income and expenses. Understanding your overall financial picture can help you make informed decisions about where to allocate your resources and how to prioritize your financial goals. Financial planning and budgeting also involve developing strategies for managing risk and protecting your assets. This might involve creating an emergency fund to cover unexpected expenses, purchasing insurance to protect your assets, or developing a diversified investment portfolio to manage risk and maximize returns. They are essential components of money management that can help you achieve your long-term financial goals, manage your day-to-day finances, and protect your assets. By developing a comprehensive financial plan and budget, you can gain greater control over your finances and build a more secure financial future.

UNDERSTANDING THE IMPORTANCE OF FINANCIAL PLANNING AND BUDGETING

Financial planning and budgeting are essential skills for anyone who wants to make money and build wealth. These skills help individuals and businesses to create a roadmap for their financial future and ensure that they are able to achieve their goals.

Financial planning involves creating a plan for how to manage your money and assets in order to achieve your long-term financial goals. This includes setting up a budget, creating an investment plan, managing debt, and creating a plan for retirement.

Budgeting is the process of creating a plan for how to spend and save money on a day-to-day basis. A budget helps you to track your income and expenses, and to ensure that you are living within your means. It can also help you to identify areas where you can cut costs and save money.

The benefits of financial planning and budgeting are numerous. First and foremost, it helps you to stay organized and focused on your financial goals. It also helps you to avoid debt and unnecessary expenses, and to make informed decisions about how to use your money.

Financial planning and budgeting also help you to prepare for unexpected events such as job loss, illness, or emergencies. By setting aside money for a rainy day, you can ensure that you are financially prepared to handle any challenges that come your way.

Finally, financial planning and budgeting help you to build wealth over time. By setting aside money for investments, retirement, and other long-term goals, you can create a solid financial foundation that will support you and your family for years to come.

DEVELOPING A BUDGET AND SETTING FINANCIAL GOALS

Developing a budget and setting financial goals are essential components of successful financial planning. A budget is a plan that outlines your income and expenses over a set period, usually monthly or yearly. It helps you track where your money is going, identify areas where you can cut back on spending, and prioritize your expenses.

To create a budget, you need to start by understanding your income and fixed expenses, such as rent or mortgage payments, car payments, and insurance premiums. Then, you should consider your variable expenses, including groceries, entertainment, and travel. Once you have a clear understanding of your income and expenses, you can determine how much you can afford to save and invest each month.

Setting financial goals is also an essential part of financial planning. A financial goal is a specific target you want to achieve within a specific period. Goals can be short-term, such as saving for a vacation, or long-term, such as saving for retirement. To set financial goals, you need to identify what you want to achieve and create a plan to reach your target.

When setting financial goals, it is essential to be realistic and specific. For example, instead of setting a general goal to save more money, you should set a specific target, such as saving $500 a month. You should also set a timeline for achieving your goals and regularly monitor your progress.

In summary, developing a budget and setting financial goals are crucial steps in financial planning. They provide a roadmap for managing your finances and help you make informed decisions about how to save and invest your money.

TRACKING EXPENSES AND MANAGING DEBT

Tracking expenses and managing debt are crucial components of financial planning and budgeting. They help individuals to gain better control of their finances, avoid unnecessary debts, and work towards achieving their financial goals.

Tracking expenses:
Tracking expenses involves recording and monitoring all money spent, including bills, groceries, rent, entertainment, and other miscellaneous expenses. This can be done manually using a spreadsheet or notebook,

or through various financial tracking apps available online.

The benefits of tracking expenses include:
- Providing a clear picture of where money is being spent
- Identifying areas where expenses can be reduced or eliminated
- Keeping individuals accountable to their financial goals
- Creating a foundation for building a realistic budget

Managing debt:
Managing debt is an important part of financial planning, as excessive debt can severely hinder an individual's financial well-being. Here are some steps to manage debt:

Create a debt payoff plan: Prioritize debts with the highest interest rates and create a plan to pay them off as soon as possible.

Negotiate lower interest rates: Contact creditors to negotiate lower interest rates on outstanding debts.

Avoid taking on new debt: Limit the use of credit cards and avoid taking on new loans until outstanding debts are paid off.

Consider debt consolidation: Consolidating multiple debts into one loan with a lower interest rate can help simplify repayment and reduce overall interest payments.

Overall, tracking expenses and managing debt are essential for building a strong financial foundation and achieving long-term financial stability.

CHAPTER 9

NEGOTIATION SKILLS

Negotiation is a skill that involves finding a mutually acceptable solution to a disagreement between two or more parties. The ability to negotiate effectively is important in both personal and professional settings, as it can help individuals reach their goals and achieve success. In order to become skilled in negotiation, there are few things you must know.

Understand the negotiation process: Negotiation typically involves several steps, including preparation, discussion, clarification of goals, proposal and counterproposal, and agreement.

Identify interests and priorities: Successful negotiation requires identifying the interests and priorities of both parties involved, and finding ways to meet those interests while still reaching a satisfactory outcome.

Effective communication: Good negotiation skills require effective communication, including active listening, asking questions, and expressing ideas clearly and persuasively.

Developing empathy and rapport: Building rapport and understanding with the other party can help create a more positive and productive negotiation process.

Creativity and problem-solving: Effective negotiation often requires creative problem-solving skills to identify new solutions and reach a mutually beneficial outcome.

Knowing when to walk away: Sometimes, negotiation simply isn't possible or isn't in your best interest. Knowing when to walk away from a negotiation is an important skill to avoid settling for an unfavorable outcome.

Negotiation in different contexts: Negotiation skills are applicable in a variety of contexts, including business, legal, and personal situations.

Developing strong negotiation skills can help individuals in various aspects of life, from closing a business deal to resolving a conflict with a loved one.

DEVELOPING EFFECTIVE NEGOTIATION SKILLS FOR SALARY, CONTRACTS AND DEALS

Negotiation is a communication process that involves two or more parties who have different interests and goals, trying to reach an agreement or settle a dispute through a discussion. Negotiation skills are an essential part of personal and professional development, especially when it comes to salary negotiations, business deals, and contract negotiations. Here are some key strategies for developing effective negotiation skills:

Prepare: Before entering into any negotiation, it's important to prepare yourself thoroughly. You should understand your own goals and interests as well as those of the other party, research the market rates or industry standards, and be aware of any alternatives or fallback options.

Active Listening: Listening actively is critical in any negotiation. By listening carefully to the other party, you can understand their needs and concerns, which will help you to find common ground and make concessions that work for both parties.

Communication Skills: Communication skills are essential for negotiation. You need to be able to clearly articulate your points and understand the other party's perspective. It is also important to use the appropriate tone, body language, and non-verbal cues to convey your message.

Creative Problem-Solving: Negotiation often involves finding creative solutions that meet the needs of both parties. You need to be open-minded and flexible in your approach, and willing to think outside the box to find solutions that work for everyone.

Emotional Intelligence: Emotions can run high in negotiations, and it's important to be able to manage your own emotions as well as those of the other party. Emotional intelligence involves being aware of your own emotions, regulating them appropriately, and being able to empathize with the other party.

Confidence: Confidence is essential in negotiation. You need to believe in the value you bring to the table, and be willing to stand up for yourself and your interests.

Persistence: Negotiation often involves a series of back-and-forth conversations, and it's important to be persistent in pursuing your goals. This doesn't mean being aggressive or confrontational, but rather being tenacious and committed to finding a solution that works for everyone.

Win-Win Mindset: Finally, successful negotiation requires a win-win mindset. You should be looking for ways to create value for both parties, rather than trying to take all the pie for yourself. This approach can lead to more positive outcomes and long-term relationships.

By mastering these strategies, you can achieve successful negotiations that benefit everyone involved.

IDENTIFYING THE OTHER PARTY'S NEEDS AND INTERESTS

Identifying the other party's needs and interests is a critical part of developing effective negotiation skills. It is essential to understand what the other party is trying to achieve and what is most important to them in the negotiation. By understanding their needs and interests, you can tailor your negotiation approach and proposals to meet their goals while still achieving your own.
Here's how to identify the other party's needs and interests

Listen carefully: Listen to what the other party is saying and ask questions to clarify their position. This will help you understand their needs and interests.

Put yourself in their shoes: Try to see the situation from the other party's perspective. What are their concerns, fears, and goals? How can you address these concerns and help them achieve their goals?
Research: Do your homework on the other party and their industry. This will give you insights into their needs and interests and help you negotiate more effectively.

Use open-ended questions: Ask open-ended questions to encourage the other party to share more about their needs and interests. For example, "What are your main concerns in this negotiation?" or "What are your goals for this project?"

Look for common ground: Identify areas of agreement and build on them. This will help create a sense of collaboration and make it easier to find a solution that works for both parties.

By understanding the other party's needs and interests, you can negotiate more effectively and increase your chances of achieving a positive outcome.

KNOWING WHEN TO WALK AWAY

Knowing when to walk away is a crucial component of effective negotiation. It is important to be able to recognize when the other party is not willing to budge on their position or is making unreasonable demands. Walking away is not necessarily a sign of weakness, but rather an indication that the negotiation has reached a stalemate and that it may be time to explore other options.

Before deciding to walk away, it is important to weigh the potential costs and benefits of continuing the negotiation versus abandoning it. This may involve considering the value of the deal or agreement being negotiated, the potential impact on future business relationships, and the costs of pursuing alternative options.

When considering walking away, it is important to communicate clearly with the other party about the reasons for doing so.

Knowing when to walk away is an important aspect of effective negotiation skills. It is not always possible to reach a deal that satisfies both parties, and sometimes it is necessary to walk away from the negotiation table. Here are some factors to consider when deciding whether to walk away from a negotiation:

The value of the deal: Consider the overall value of the deal being negotiated. If the deal is not worth the effort, time, or resources being invested, it may be better to walk away.

Alternatives: Consider the availability of alternative options. If there are other viable options, it may be easier to walk away from the current negotiation.

Time constraints: Consider whether there are any time constraints involved in the negotiation. If time is running out and a deal cannot be reached, it may be necessary to walk away.

Personal values: Consider whether the negotiation aligns with your personal values and ethics. If the deal requires compromising your values, it may be best to walk away.

Relationship with the other party: Consider the relationship with the other party. If the negotiation is causing damage to the relationship, it may be better to walk away rather than risk further damage.

Ultimately, the decision to walk away from a negotiation is a personal one and should be based on a careful consideration of the factors involved. Effective negotiation skills involve being able to assess the situation objectively and make informed decisions based on the available information.

CHAPTER 10

BUILDING A PERSONAL BRAND

Building a personal brand involves creating a unique image and reputation for oneself that showcases their skills, values, and personality. This personal brand can be used to establish credibility, increase visibility, and attract opportunities such as job offers, collaborations, and sponsorships. Here are some key details on building a personal brand:

Determine your niche: Identify your strengths, skills, and interests, and determine what sets you apart from others in your field. This will help you define your unique selling proposition (USP) and establish yourself as an expert in your area.

Create a consistent online presence: Develop a strong and consistent presence on social media platforms, blogs, and other online platforms. Use a consistent tone, voice, and messaging across all platforms, and ensure that your online presence aligns with your personal brand and values.

Engage with your audience: Engage with your audience regularly, by responding to comments and messages, sharing valuable content, and providing insights and expertise. This will help you build a community of followers and establish yourself as a thought leader in your area.

Network and collaborate: Attend events, join online groups and communities, and collaborate with other professionals in your field. This will help you expand your network, gain exposure, and build your personal brand.

Invest in your personal development: Continuously learn and grow, attend conferences and workshops, and invest in your personal and professional development. This will help you stay up-to-date with the latest trends and developments in your field, and position yourself as a valuable asset in your industry.

Overall, building a personal brand takes time and effort, but can pay off in the long run by helping you establish a strong reputation, gain visibility, and attract opportunities.

UNDERSTANDING THE IMPORTANCE OF PERSONAL BRANDING

Personal branding is the process of establishing and promoting an individual's unique identity, image, and reputation in a way that sets them apart from others. It is the way you market yourself, the image you create, and the value you offer to others. It involves identifying your unique skills, strengths, values, and personality traits, and then developing a strategy to communicate those qualities to your target audience.

Having a strong personal brand is becoming increasingly important in today's competitive job market and business world. It can help you stand out from the crowd, establish credibility and trust with potential clients or employers, and increase your opportunities for career advancement or business growth.

To build a strong personal brand, it is important to start by defining your unique value proposition – what sets you apart from others in your industry or field. This can be based on your skills, experience, personality, or any other distinguishing factor. You should also identify your target audience and understand their needs and preferences.

Once you have defined your value proposition and target audience, you can start building your personal brand through various channels such as social media, blogs, public speaking, networking events, and more. Consistency is key – you should use the same messaging, visual branding, and tone of voice across all channels to create a cohesive and recognizable brand.

It is also important to monitor and manage your personal brand over time. This includes regularly reviewing your online presence, responding to feedback and criticism, and making adjustments to your brand strategy as needed. Building a strong personal brand requires time, effort, and a clear understanding of your unique value proposition and target audience. But the rewards can be significant, including increased visibility, credibility, and opportunities for career or business growth.

IDENTIFYING YOUR UNIQUE SELLING POINTS

Identifying your unique selling points (USPs) is an essential step in building a strong personal brand. Your USPs are the characteristics, qualities, and skills that make you stand out from the crowd and differentiate you from others in your field.

Here are some tips for identifying your USPs:

Know your strengths: Take time to identify your unique talents, skills, and expertise. What do you do better than others in your field?

Identify your passions: Your personal brand should reflect your passions and values. What motivates you and gets you excited about your work?

Research your competition: Look at others in your field and identify what sets you apart from them. What do you offer that they don't?

Identify your target audience: Who are you trying to reach with your personal brand? What are their needs and desires? How can you meet those needs better than anyone else?

Get feedback: Ask your colleagues, clients, and friends for feedback on your strengths and what they see as your unique selling points.

Once you have identified your USPs, make sure to incorporate them into your personal brand messaging, whether it's on your website, social media profiles, or other marketing materials. Your USPs should be a central part of your brand and the value you offer to your audience.

DEVELOPING AN ONLINE PRESENCE AND REPUTATION

Developing an online presence and reputation is a crucial part of building a personal brand in today's digital age. Here are some details on how to do it effectively:

Define your personal brand: Before you start creating an online presence, it's important to define your personal brand. This includes identifying your values, mission, and unique selling proposition. It will help you stay consistent in your messaging and content across all platforms.

Choose your online platforms: There are a variety of online platforms available to build your personal brand, including social media, blogs, podcasts, and personal websites. Choose the platforms that best align with your brand and target audience.

Create valuable content: Developing high-quality content is a critical part of building your online presence. Create content that aligns with your personal brand and provides value to your audience. This could include blog posts, social media updates, podcasts, videos, or online courses.

Engage with your audience: Building relationships with your audience is essential for growing your personal brand. Engage with your audience by responding to comments, participating in online communities, and hosting live events.

Maintain a consistent brand image: Consistency is key when it comes to building a personal brand. Use the same profile picture, color scheme, and messaging across all platforms to establish a consistent brand image.

Monitor your online reputation: It's important to regularly monitor your online reputation and respond to any negative feedback or comments. Responding professionally and authentically can help turn a negative situation into a positive one.

Continuously refine and improve your brand: Building a personal brand is an ongoing process. Continuously refine and improve your brand by regularly evaluating your goals and metrics, and adjusting your strategy as necessary.

By following these steps, you can effectively develop an online presence and reputation that aligns with your personal brand and helps you achieve your goals.

CHAPTER 11

NETWORKING AND BUILDING CONNECTIONS

Networking and building connections is an important aspect of building a personal brand and establishing a successful career or business. It involves building relationships with people in your industry, community, or other relevant fields, with the goal of establishing mutually beneficial connections and opportunities. Effective networking and building connections requires a combination of online and offline efforts, as well as a willingness to invest time and effort in building relationships with others.

Here are some ways to effectively network and build connections:

Attend networking events: Look for events, conferences, or trade shows related to your field or interests. Attend these events and use them as an opportunity to meet new people, exchange business cards, and make connections.

Join professional organizations: Joining professional organizations related to your industry or field can provide you with networking opportunities, as well as access to valuable resources, industry news, and training and development programs.

Use social media: Social media platforms like LinkedIn, Twitter, and Facebook can be useful tools for building connections and establishing an online presence. Follow industry leaders, participate in online discussions, and share content that showcases your expertise.

Reach out to existing contacts: Don't be afraid to reach out to former colleagues, classmates, or other contacts to catch up and see if there are any potential networking opportunities or collaborations.

Be genuine and authentic: Building connections is about building relationships, so it's important to be genuine and authentic in your interactions. Listen to others, show interest in their work, and offer your help or expertise when appropriate.

Reach Out to People: Don't be afraid to reach out to people you admire or respect. Introduce yourself and ask if they would be willing to meet for coffee or have a quick chat over the phone. Be genuine and show interest in their work.

Offer Value: Building relationships is a two-way street. Offer value to the people you are connecting with by sharing your knowledge, skills, or resources. This can help you establish yourself as a valuable and trustworthy connection.

Follow Up: After meeting someone new, follow up with them to stay in touch. Send a quick email or message thanking them for their time and express your interest in staying connected.

Networking and building connections is a continuous process that requires effort, patience, and consistency.

THE IMPORTANCE OF BUILDING CONNECTIONS IN BUSINESS

Building connections is an essential aspect of business success. It involves creating and nurturing relationships with individuals and organizations that can provide support, resources, and opportunities for growth. Here are some of the reasons why building connections is crucial in business:

Access to resources: Connections can provide access to resources that can help a business grow, such as funding, talent, and technology. Building connections with investors, industry experts, and other entrepreneurs can increase the chances of finding the right resources at the right time.

Learning opportunities: Building connections also provides opportunities to learn from others. By engaging with experts in the industry or peers, entrepreneurs can gain insights and knowledge that can help them improve their business operations and make better decisions.

Opportunities for collaboration: Connections can lead to collaborations that can benefit all parties involved. By working with other businesses or individuals, entrepreneurs can leverage each other's strengths to achieve common goals.

Referrals and recommendations: Strong connections can lead to referrals and recommendations from trusted sources, which can be invaluable for growing a business. Word-of-mouth marketing can be a powerful tool, and having a network of people who are willing to recommend your business can help attract new customers.

Increased visibility: Building connections can also increase visibility for a business. By networking and building relationships with individuals and organizations in the industry, entrepreneurs can increase their visibility and establish themselves as experts in their field.

Building connections is a critical component of business success. It requires time and effort, but the benefits can be significant, from access to resources and learning opportunities to collaborations and increased visibility.

DEVELOPING A PROFESSIONAL NETWORK

Developing a professional network is important for building a successful career and business. A professional network is a group of individuals who can provide you with information, support, and advice. They can also help you make connections with potential clients, customers, and business partners.

Here are some steps you can take to develop your professional network:

Attend industry events: Attend industry events such as conferences, seminars, and trade shows to meet people in your field. These events provide opportunities to learn about industry trends, exchange ideas, and make new connections.

Join professional organizations: Joining professional organizations related to your field can help you build relationships with other professionals. These organizations often have networking events and can provide access to job listings and other resources.

Connect with people on social media: Social media platforms like LinkedIn provide opportunities to connect with other professionals in your field. You can join groups related to your industry, share your work and accomplishments, and connect with people who may be interested in your services.

Participate in online forums: Participating in online forums and discussion boards related to your field can help you connect with other professionals and stay up-to-date on industry news and trends.

Reach out to people you admire: Don't be afraid to reach out to people you admire or respect in your field. You can send a friendly message or email introducing yourself and expressing your admiration for their work. This can lead to valuable connections and even mentorship opportunities.

Follow up: After making new connections, make sure to follow up with them. Send a thank-you note or email, or invite them to connect on LinkedIn. Staying in touch can help you maintain these connections and keep your professional network active.

TIPS FOR NETWORKING EFFECTIVELY

Here are some tips for networking effectively:
- **Identify your target audience:** Before attending a networking event or reaching out to someone, identify the type of person or industry you want to connect with.
- **Make a great first impression:** Dress appropriately, smile, make eye contact, and

have a firm handshake. Be confident and positive.

- ❖ **Be prepared:** Have business cards, a clear introduction, and a brief pitch about what you do and what you can offer.
- ❖ **Listen and ask questions:** Show genuine interest in others by asking questions and actively listening to their responses.
- ❖ **Follow up:** After the event, send a follow-up email or message to thank them for their time and reiterate your interest in connecting further.
- ❖ **Offer value:** Focus on how you can help others rather than just what you can get out of the relationship. Offer advice or share resources that may be helpful to them.
- ❖ **Attend events and join organizations:** Join relevant professional organizations, attend events, and participate in online communities to expand your network.

Remember that networking is about building long-term relationships, not just exchanging business cards. It requires time and effort, but the payoff can be significant in terms of new opportunities and connections.

CHAPTER 12

In conclusion, making money is not always an easy feat, but it is achievable with the right mindset, knowledge, and effort. This book has provided valuable insights into various ways to make money, including investing in stocks, real estate, freelancing, online businesses, and passive income streams. It has also highlighted the importance of financial planning, negotiation skills, personal branding, and networking in achieving financial success. By following the advice and tips provided in this book, anyone can take steps towards creating a more prosperous and financially stable future. Remember that making money requires patience, discipline, and a willingness to take calculated risks. With persistence and hard work, anyone can achieve their financial goals and live the life they desire.

It Is crucial to remember that making money is not a get-rich-quick scheme; it takes patience, hard work, and perseverance. With the right mindset and a willingness to learn and adapt, anyone can develop the skills and knowledge necessary to make money and secure their financial future.

BRINGING TOGETHER THE VARIOUS STRATEGIES DISCUSSED IN THIS BOOK

Throughout this book, we have explored a variety of strategies for making money, including investing in stocks and real estate, freelancing and consulting, building online businesses, creating passive income, developing negotiation skills, and building a personal brand and professional network.

While each of these strategies is unique and requires its own set of skills and knowledge, they all share some common principles. For example, successful money-making strategies often require a combination of hard work, patience, and smart decision-making. Additionally, most strategies require an initial investment of time, money, or both, and it is important to carefully consider the risks and potential rewards of any investment.

Another important theme that runs throughout this book is the importance of continuous learning and adaptation. In today's rapidly changing economy, the strategies that worked well in the past may not be as effective in the future, and it is essential to stay up-to-date with industry trends and developments.

Ultimately, the key to making money is to find a strategy that aligns with your unique skills, interests, and goals, and to approach it with a mindset of determination, flexibility, and a willingness to learn and adapt. By applying the principles discussed in this book, you can take steps to build a successful and fulfilling career that will help you achieve your financial aspirations.

DEVELOPING A PERSONAL PLAN FOR MAKING MONEY

Developing a personal plan for making money is the culmination of the various strategies discussed in the book. This involves taking an individualized approach to combining the various methods and strategies that have been covered, and tailoring them to one's own skills, interests, and resources.

The first step In developing a personal plan for making money is to identify one's financial goals and priorities. This could include short-term goals, such as paying off debt or saving for a down payment on a house, as well as long-term goals, such as building a retirement nest egg or starting a business.

Once financial goals have been established, the next step is to evaluate one's skills and interests to identify the most viable income-generating opportunities. This could involve further developing skills through education or training, or leveraging existing skills to create new income streams.

From there, it is important to explore the various income-generating strategies covered in the book, such as investing in stocks, real estate, or other assets, building a freelance or consulting business, or creating passive income streams through rental properties, investments, or digital products.

With a solid understanding of these various strategies, individuals can then develop a personalized plan that combines the most appropriate methods for their own unique situation. This plan should include specific action steps, timelines, and measurable goals to help ensure success.

In conclusion, developing a personal plan for making money requires a combination of self-reflection, strategic thinking, and practical action steps. By leveraging the various strategies discussed in the book and tailoring them to one's own needs and resources, anyone can take meaningful steps towards achieving their financial goals and securing their financial future.

TIPS FOR MAINTAINING SUCCESS AND CONTINUING TO GROW FINANCIALLY.

Maintaining success and continuing to grow financially is crucial for long-term financial stability and independence. Here are some tips for achieving this:

❖ **Continuously learn and adapt:** The financial landscape is constantly changing, and it is important to stay informed and adapt accordingly. Read books, attend

seminars, and seek out new opportunities to learn and grow.
- **Diversify your income streams:** Relying on a single source of income can be risky. Consider diversifying your income streams by investing in multiple areas, developing passive income streams, or pursuing side hustles.
- **Maintain a budget and track your expenses:** Even when you start making more money, it is important to maintain a budget and track your expenses to ensure you are staying within your means and not overspending.
- **Save and invest wisely:** Make sure you are saving and investing your money wisely by considering the risks and rewards of each investment opportunity. Seek advice from professionals if necessary.
- **Set and revisit financial goals regularly:** Setting and revisiting financial goals regularly can help keep you motivated and on track. Celebrate your achievements and adjust your goals as necessary to keep pushing yourself forward.

❖ By following these tips, you can maintain your financial success and continue to grow your wealth over time.

How to make money

www.ingramcontent.com/pod-product-compliance
Lightning Source LLC
Chambersburg PA
CBHW031534210526
45464CB00013B/507